THE MOON IS NOT THE SON

THE MOON IS NOT THE SON

A close look at the teachings of
REV. SUN MYUNG MOON
and the **UNIFICATION CHURCH**

By James Bjornstad

15338

DIMENSION BOOKS
BETHANY FELLOWSHIP, INC.
Minneapolis, Minnesota

The Moon Is Not the Son
by James Bjornstad

Library of Congress Catalog Card Number
76-46208

ISBN 0-87123-380-0

DIMENSION BOOKS
Published by Bethany Fellowship, Inc.
6820 Auto Club Road,
Minneapolis, Minnesota 55438

Printed in the United States of America

DEDICATED

to my students at Northeastern
Bible College who never cease
to amaze me by finding some
new religious movement or
practice, and then desiring that
I tell them what it's all about and
how they can reach these people
for Jesus Christ.

JAMES BJORNSTAD is executive director of the Institute of Contemporary Christianity, and instructor in Philosophy and Theology at Northeastern Bible College. He attended City College of New York, received two degrees from Northeastern Bible College (B.R.E., Th.B.), received his Master's Degree in Religious Education from New York Theological Seminary, and has completed his course work for a Ph.D. from New York University.

Among his previously published works are *Twentieth-Century Prophecy* and *The Transcendental Mirage.*

He is a member of the Evangelical Theological Society and the Society of Biblical Literature and Exegesis.

Mr. Bjornstad has done thirteen years of research and study on the religious movements and practices in America. He has also had four years of college teaching experience in the area. His lectures on the subject have taken him to universities, conferences and churches throughout America.

The Moon Is Not the Son culminates more than three years of intensive research, dialogue and continuous interaction with the Unification Church, its leaders and its theology.

Preface

It was a beautiful autumn day. I had just finished teaching at Northeastern Bible College and was on my way home. I stopped for a few moments at the Willowbrook Shopping Center, where I was approached by two neatly dressed young men, one trying to sell me candy, and the other votive light candles. They assured me that my purchase would be a contribution for a worthy cause— for missionary work and the support of orphans (which I am certainly not opposed to). I asked them what organization I would be giving to, and the reply was "a fine Christian organization." I attempted to pursue the identity of this organization, but with little success. Finally I noted a large black book in with the supplies one of them had, and I asked if I could see it. Relunctantly, he let me glance through it. It was titled *Divine Principle*. As I opened the pages, I discovered the name of the organization—The Holy Spirit Association for the Unification of World Christianity, or the Unification Church, as it is commonly referred to. As I thumbed through the volume, I began to notice its theology. It disturbed me. Teaching in the fields of philosophy and theology as I do helped me immensely in analyzing their teachings. I began to ask some questions about statements in the *Divine Principle,* which only resulted in the termination of our conversation. So I continued on to the store and then home.

When I arrived home I sat down to eat my dinner. I barely got a bite of food when the doorbell rang. A very pleasant young man greeted me with a big smile and handed me a flyer which had the words "Christianity in Crisis—New Hope—Sun Myung Moon." It was an invitation to attend a lecture by Rev. Moon at Madison Square Garden. By the time I finished reading the flyer, the young man was already several houses away, passing out flyers as he went. So I went back and finished my dinner.

Then the telephone rang, and a Christian friend was calling to see if my wife and I would like to attend an evangelistic crusade. He had invited several non-Christian neighbors and friends to go and hear this evangelist from Korea, the Reverend Sun Myung Moon. I couldn't believe it. So I began to tell him parts of Rev. Moon's theology. He was shocked.

Three encounters in one day was enough to tell me I needed to learn more about this Rev. Moon, his theology and his church. Prior to that day I knew nothing about him. I had not even heard his name. But since that day, I have spent many hours in researching this new religious movement in America.

On the one hand, my research has involved interviews with many members of the Unification Church, as well as a few ex-members. On the other hand, I have presented several lectures on Rev. Moon's theology for universities, community groups, churches and conferences. The question period at the conclusion of my presentations have been most helpful in refining my thinking, as well as in defending my analysis, regarding this movement.

I wish to express my sincere thanks to all who have been interviewed, as well as to many who have just taken the time to sit and talk with me about this entire subject. I appreciate also those who have questioned me and some who have challenged me regarding my analysis. It has all had a part in the final formulation of this material.

My special thanks to two pastors: Rev. John Koppenaal, pastor of the First Baptist Church of Rhinebeck, New York, and Rev. Michael D. Redmond, pastor of the Valley Road Covenant Church in Montclair, New Jersey. These two men took time out from their busy schedules to help me with my research. My appreciation also to Dr. Ernest J. Giovanoli, a psychiatrist in Rhinebeck, New York, who helped me understand the "brainwashing" techniques used by the Unification Church.

Just as I had my first encounter with the followers of Rev. Moon on that lovely autumn day several years ago, so also today there are many who are being approached by their selling team or witnessing team—without any idea of what it's all about.

I am also concerned for the members of the Unification Church, many of whom have never honestly considered the real claims regarding the person and work of the Lord Jesus Christ; their only knowledge of it being that which has been told to them by the Unification Church.

It is with all these people in mind that this book has been written, with the prayer that it will help each reader to understand what the Unification Church is all about, to discern the truth from the false among the religious movements today, and to discover that truth in a personal relationship with the Lord Jesus Christ, "Our Great God and Savior" (Titus 2:13).

Table of Contents

Acknowledgments

My sincerest thanks to Joseph Bataglia, editor of *Alternatives* magazine, for his permission to include the testimony "Why I Left the Unification Church" in the appendices of this volume; and also to Michael Scott for his permission to publish his testimony with the prayer that it would be of help to others.

Key

to abbreviations of sources
used in footnotes

DP = *Divine Principle* (Washington, D.C.: The Holy Spirit Association for the Unification of World Christianity, 1973)

DPA = Young Oon Kim, *The Divine Principle and Its Application* (Belvedere Tarrytown, New York: The Holy Spirit Association for the Unification of World Christianity, n.d.)

DPSG = *The Divine Principle Study Guide* (Belvedere Tarrytown, New York: The Holy Spirit Association for the Unification of World Christianity, May 1, 1973)

PC = Young Whi Kim, *The Principle of Creation* (Belvedere Tarrytown, New York: The Holy Spirit Association for the Unification of World Christianity, March 15, 1973)

UT = *Unification Thought* (New York, New York: Unification Thought Institute, 1973)

UTCT = Young Oon Kim, *Unification Theology & Christian Thought* (New York: Golden Gate Publishing Co., 1975)

UTSG = *Unification Thought Study Guide* (New York, New York: Unification Thought Institute, January 30, 1974)

Introduction

Start with a well-seasoned Taoist philosophy, add plenty of Christian words and phrases, and even some Bible verses, and stir briskly until they blend together. Now add a bit of spiritism, not too much mysticism, a pinch of numerology, a dab of physics and a dash of anti-communism; mix it all together using a Korean Messiah until it blends, and you have the recipe for one of the new religious movements sweeping across America—The Unification Church founded by Rev. Sun Myung Moon.

This church was founded in 1954 in Korea and has become popular here in the United States since 1972. It claims to have over three million followers in 120 countries, with about 30,000 members in America, some 10,000 of these living in its religious communities.

The members of this church are sacrificial people, and there's no denying their dedication and enthusiasm. Most of them are clean-cut, bright-faced young people in their twenties.

They have been referred to as Moonies, Moonites, Moon people, Moonflowers Moonweeds, Moon children, and Moonbeams. (People seem to have a field day playing with Rev. Moon's name.) In the same manner his followers have been looked upon as Moon-merized, Moonwashed and Moonstruck; and their fund-raising activities as Moonlighting.

You have probably met or seen some of these young people without realizing who they were. They usually keep their identity in the background when selling their wares —everything from pamphlets, peanuts, candy and candles to American flags, flowers and terrariums. They will either tell you your purchase was for "a good cause," or else ask you for a donation for "missionary work," "support of orphans," "research for the blind," "helping to combat the drug problem," etc.—everything short of the real reason. It all goes to support the Unification Church and its activities.

Some of the members actually delight in practicing this "heavenly deception," as they refer to it. As one member explained, "Satan deceived God's children, so we are justified in deceiving Satan's children." In a few instances this deception has brought about embarrassing situations for the Unification Church. In Burlington, Vermont, members of the fund-raising team of the church were out on the streets soliciting funds for a "King Street youth center." Since this selling team was comprised of out-of-staters sent in for the occasion, they had no idea that there really was such a center on King Street. When picketing young people appeared in front of the Unification center protesting this misrepresentation, the church's leaders were embarrassed, but quickly recovered to rationalize away the lie by saying that these members were "confused" about the center's address.[1]

The followers of Rev. Moon can also be seen in a variety of other activities, such as singing choruses of hope in subway stations and bus terminals, cleaning up streets or public areas, giving lectures on street corners, and blitzing cities with literature for Rev. Moon's speaking engagements. In these endeavors, one can usually figure out from what they say or from the literature they pass out that it is the Unification Church. Sometimes they will even wear badges identifying themselves as a member of the Unification Church.

It is also possible that you might have had contact with one or more of the organizations, companies or other groups in the United States which are controlled by or affiliated with Rev. Moon and the Unification Church. Very few of these relationships have been made public. These include such known affiliations as One World Crusade, International Federation for Victory over Communism, American Youth for a Just Peace, Freedom Leadership Foundation, the Little Angels of Korea Folk Ballet, the International Conference on Unified Science and others. And then there are those of which we're not even aware.

A few years ago, a strong evangelical leader, Dr. Bob Jones III, out of "compassion and concern for Korean children," became a member of the Advisory Board of the Korean Cultural and Freedom Foundation, Inc. He was on that board for three or four months before he discovered that it was an affiliation of the Unification Church. Upon learning this he promptly resigned.[2] This could happen to anyone because of all the mystery that engulfs these relationships.

Most people, however, are familiar with this group and Rev. Moon because of the great deal of adverse publicity they are drawing from the media—such as 1) alleged "kidnappings" and "brainwashing" of young people and subsequent "re-kidnappings" by their parents and "de-programming"; 2) investigation of the church by the Internal Revenue Service and some problems with the U.S. Naturalization and Immigration Service; 3) revelation of their behind-the-scene pressure on American politicians (e.g., the church's assigning several young ladies to each Senator and Congressman in Washington); 4) portraying Rev. Moon as a Korean Elmer Gantry living luxuriously from his followers sacrificial earnings; 5) questioning his close ties with South Korean dictator Park Chung Hee whose government has sent hundreds of Christians and other religious leaders to jail in the past few years, but never bothers Rev. Moon's disciples there; and 6) making public his avowed "World Dictatorship" statements to his inner circle (e.g., "There is a day coming when what I say will be the law of the land." "The whole world is in my hand. I will conquer and subjugate the world.").

Although usually silent in responding to the reports of the media (at least publicly), with the exception of comments by the church's president, Neil Albert Salonen, the church has recently begun a response in a positive fashion. Instead of criticizing her critics regarding the alleged destruction of lives through "brainwashing" in the church's training program, the church took out a one-page ad in the *New York Times* and printed excerpts from letters of parents and friends stressing the good that has been done in many lives and demonstrating the worth and the value of Rev. Moon's theology and the church's training for young lives.[3]

Part of the "public image" of this group is also due to several anti-Moon organizations which have come into existence all with the avowed purpose of opposing Rev. Moon and the Unification Church. Rabbi Maurice Davis heads up a 500+ family national organization called Citizens Engaged in Reuniting Families. But the most fervent foes are the ex-devotees. Three of these have founded the International Foundation for Individual Freedom, and another is involved in Christians United for Jesus as Lord.

The most natural questions in the midst of all of this publicity is "Who's telling the truth?" and "What in the world is going on with that group?" Still others want to know, "Who is this Sun Myung Moon? Where did he come from? What are his claims to fame? What are they doing to our young people? Why are our young people joining his movement? What does he believe and what is he teaching these people?"

In addition to the above, the *Bible* also raises some questions for consideration. The Apostle John was concerned with those who would claim to be God's messengers but in reality were not. He provided a test in 1 John 4 to help us determine God's messengers from those who are not. If we put Rev. Moon to John's test, is he a true messenger of God as he claims? Likewise, the Apostle Paul was concerned that someone might come and deceive the Christian Church by teaching about "another Jesus," bringing "another gospel" and being em-

15338

powered by "another spirit" (2 Cor. 11). If we examine Rev. Moon in the light of Paul's concern, what will we find? What Jesus does he present? Does he have another gospel? Is there another spirit other than that of the Holy Spirit empowering his ministry? Paul reminds us in that same chapter that these counterfeits can appear to be "ministers of righteousness," and that this fact should not be surprising because Satan himself appears as an "angel of light."

With all of these questions before us, our task in this book will be to provide some basic information which should help you to understand, discern and evaluate this religious movement. It should help you answer the questions, and also provide a basis for further investigation should you desire to do so. Bear in mind that no one study, regardless of the time spent in research and the thoroughness of the investigation, can cover and examine all areas of any religious movement.

Thus we propose to begin by tracing the historical background of the Unification Church and Rev. Moon. Then we will look at the theology, contrasting it with biblical theology, since both the Unification Church and Rev. Moon claim to be a continuation of the biblical tradition. We will conclude by examining the claims of Rev. Moon and his theology.

In the presentation that follows, the evidence has been examined as carefully as possible. The conclusions have been drawn from evidence, most of which is accessible for anyone to consider.

1

Moon's History Presented

He "orates in a raspy shout, goose-steps across the stage and slashes the air with karate chops," says one writer trying to describe the phenomena he had just witnessed—a new religious figure on the American scene, the Rev. Sun Myung Moon.

Young Myung Moon (loosely translated "Shining Dragon Moon") was born in a Presbyterian family on January 6, 1920, in the Pyungan Buk-do province of what is now North Korea. (His name was later changed to Sun Myung Moon.)

From his earliest childhood he has always been interested in spiritism, but it was not until he was 16 years old that his first important encounter occurred. That was on an Easter Sunday morning in 1936 when Jesus appeared to him while he was in prayer and "revealed that he was destined to accomplish a great mission in which Jesus would work with him." [1] Some say that he was actually told to restore God's perfect kingdom, while others say he was told by Jesus that he would be "the completer of man's salvation by being the Second Coming of Christ." (Not much is said in detail of this experience, probably because Rev. Moon's experiences in the 1940s really set forth the basis for his teachings and authority.)

Visits from the spirit world and other spiritualistic phenomena play no small part in Rev. Moon's life and theology. It is an integral part. Rev. Moon continually receives "new revelations," practices a form of soul travel whereby he allegedly projects himself into the spirit realm to see Jesus and the saints, and claims to be an "expert" on the spirit world.

In the seven years following this initial experience of importance, the contents of the *Divine Principle* were developed, according to his followers. (Actually this development continued beyond this period at least through 1945.) During this time he was a student in the field of electrical engineering in Japan, and also a student of the Bible on his own. The latter, of course, provided the basis for his reworking of the Bible.

After World War II, while living in North Korea, he became involved in an underground Pentecostal movement of an extreme nature in Pyong Yang. This group was deeply entrenched in mystical revelations, awaiting the impending appearance of a new Messiah. They believed that Korea was the New Jerusalem of the Bible and that the Messiah would be born in Korea (all elements which are found in Rev. Moon's theology and in the *Divine Principle*).

In 1945, probably as a culmination of the experiences in the above group, Rev. Moon had his most important experience. He tells us of this in *Master Speaks,* but perhaps the most succinct statement of it is found in the claims of the Unification Church itself:

> At that moment, he became the absolute victor of heaven and earth. The whole spirit world bowed down to him on that day of victory . . . The spirit world has already recognized him as the victor of the universe and the Lord of creation.[2]

The *Divine Principle* mentions this experience by saying that "he fought alone against myriads of satanic forces, both in the spirit and physical world, and finally triumphed over them all." [3]

As a result of this experience, he changed his birth name to Sun Myung Moon which means "Shining Sun and Moon"— a title savoring of divinity and of the whole universe.

Following this, while still residing in North Korea, Rev. Moon was sent to jail. His followers say that it was because of his anti-communism, while others say it was for bigamy and adultery. A former North Korean army officer who was in prison with Rev. Moon says that Moon received a seven-year sentence for contributing to "social disorder," proclaiming the imminent coming of the second messiah in Korea. [4]

He was released from jail in 1950 when the United Nations forces under General Douglas MacArthur entered North Korea. He moved down to Pusan in South Korea, where he became a harbor laborer. In 1954 he founded his church in Seoul: it was officially called the Holy Spirit Association for the Unification of World Christianity.

In the same year his first wife left him. "She did not understand my religion," Rev. Moon explains.

In 1955 he was arrested and placed in jail again, this time in South Korea. The government charged him with draft evasion and later with adultery and promiscuity (the latter stemming from claims about his ritual sex with women in his church). His followers explain how the moral charges occurred by stating that in the early years of the church, meetings were held in the homes of his followers, most of whom were women. Because the meetings would go until the early hours of the morning, rumors began to develop and spread that these were affairs.

On the other side, Rev. Won II Chei, a leading Presbyterian minister in Seoul, says, "If we believe those who have gone into this group and come out, they say that one has to receive Sun Myung Moon's blood to receive salvation. That blood is ordinarily received by three periods of sexual intercourse." [5]

One long-time follower of Rev. Moon added an interesting sidelight to this. He said, "It is entirely possible that those sexual rituals were a part of the early church in Korea. Since original sin came through the woman's [Eve's] intercourse with Lucifer through which she received his evil characteristics, it is perfectly logical that the reversal of this, woman's intercourse with the perfect man through which she could receive his perfect characteristics, would liquidate original sin. Then, as Adam received Satan's evil characteristics from Eve through intercourse, so man would receive perfect characteristics through intercourse with the woman."

Whatever the reason, the government failed to prove its case against Rev. Moon. Thus the Unification Church can say, as W. Farley Jones, director of its Public Information Office, did in his letter to the *Christian Century* magazine, that the morals charges were dropped and that the "Korean Court records document this." [6]

The year 1957 brought about the publication of the *Divine Principle*, a volume written not by Rev. Moon, as many people think, but by one of his followers, Yee Hye Wen. This is the "key to the Scriptures" of the Unification Church, their theological interpretation of the Bible. This volume sets forth Moon's teachings to his disciples in Korea, and, as the *Divine Principle* itself states, it is only "part of the truth." [7]

Some within the church have indicated that there are areas which need refining and reworking in the *Divine Principle,* such as the statement that there are many direct parallels between the "Babylonian Captivities" (i.e., a comparison of Israel and Judah's fate under the Babylonians, with the Papal problems of the Roman Catholic Church in the fourteenth and fifteenth centuries).[8] Some have indicated that a whole new volume is needed.

It is interesting to note that regarding the English translations alone, the second edition (1973) is different from the first edition (1966) in quite a few areas. Any comparison of these two editions would easily reveal this.

In the years that followed, Rev. Moon developed his business enterprises, which included gingseng tea, titanium products, pharmaceuticals and air rifles. He became a wealthy man, and as his wealth increased so did his standing in the community. Finally in the mid 1960s he launched a vigorous campaign against communism which brought him the support of South Korea's leader, Park Chung Hee.

January 1, 1972, was a major turning

point in the ministry of his church. God appeared to him and told him to come to America for the purpose of preparing the people here for the second advent of Christ. A 22-acre estate in Tarrytown, New York, was purchased as the American headquarters, providing an elaborate training center for his followers as well as a mansion for his family.

Rev. Moon then launched out into America by way of rallies and crusades. His performance was always in Korean and was complicated by the fact that his translator also was very difficult to understand because of his own thick accent. Perhaps this is the reason so many people would leave part way through his lectures.

In 1974 he began to speak out stronger on behalf of America, and especially on behalf of the President, Richard Nixon. In fact, he led a pro-Nixon rally on the steps of the Nation's capitol. In other cities his followers also held similar rallies. But it was not long afterward that Nixon resigned.

From America an international emphasis was initiated in 1975. Rev. Moon assigned three missionaries to each of ninety-five new countries. Furthermore, crusade teams would be sent out on three-month tours beginning with four selected countries.[9]

The Unification Church has quite a history of rejections in its quest for approval by religious councils and groups. From Korea to America, the trail includes the Presbyterian Church in Korea, a Korean Council of Churches and several council of churches here in America, including some for whom this rejection was their very first refusal of anyone. There are also some denominations which have spoken out against the Unification Church by way of resolutions or other statements. As far as we can tell, none accepted them.

In spite of this the Unification Church continues to attract people. Young people between 17 and 30 especially find this religious movement appealing. From conversations with converts it seems that these young people find therein an alternative life-style that does not demand sexual performance, radical politics or drug participation; yet it allows them to live in a commune, work hard and hope to improve the lot of fellowman. Some are inspired by messianic hopes that their children will not have to grow up and live in a world like this one, but as perfected children under the Lord of the Second Advent.

Controversy reigns over these converts to Rev. Moon. More than 1,000 families throughout the United States have contacted the Dutchess County District Attorney regarding their children who have gone into the Unification Church, complaining of some type of mind control or mind influence over their child. Many ex-members of the church have testified that this was the case with them.

One interesting example involves a newspaper reporter working under cover. He went to one of the centers and joined a group. During his stay there he found himself overwhelmed. It got through to him and he found himself confessing to one of the other initiates that he was a reporter. His remarks are interesting and bear out the effectiveness of their training program: "How could it happen, I thought. I had been there two and a half days. I found Moon's principles unbelievable. Yet I suddenly fell off guard." [10]

To understand the process of what actually happens at these centers, one should read the article on "Brainwashing" in the *Encyclopaedia Britannica*. Though not written on the Unification Church, one can easily note the various stages involved in breaking down the ego structure. With any knowledge of the actions and activities in a center, the article relates to and identifies that which is used by the Unification Church.

Years ago involuntary conversion was achieved through physical coercion. Torture of this nature is still in force today, as a recent *Time* magazine article brought out.[11] But in the past few decades a new method is being used to bring about this conversion. It is psychological coercion, which is the means used in Unification centers. The first step is isolation, where one is removed from the usual cultural support system of his or her pattern of behavior. To prevent one from leaving the new environment, they use psychology: "How can you forsake us and leave? We love you so very much." (This is called "love bombing.") Or, "Satan is trying to pull you away from God because you have been called and chosen to build the Kingdom of heaven. Don't give in to Satan."

The second step is willingness, which is usually already accomplished because the person freely comes to the center. From here on it is only a matter of producing thought control or brainwashing in a controlled social environment, one in which the initiate conforms to the group's perception of reality. The person's identity is conformed to that of the group. So completely is this accomplished that the following account by an ex-Moonie only begins to reveal the great transformation. After being de-programmed, she said, "Adjusting to the outside world again was like arriving on another planet. Driving my car, balancing my checkbook, watching TV and reading books besides Moon's *Divine Principle* were strange. It took a long time to fill the vacuum that had been created inside me." [12]

One of the representatives of the Unification Church explained the above procedure by saying, "It is not brainwashing. It's purely a system of indoctrination, the same as you Christians use." Well, let it be clearly understood that what the Unification Church does is more than indoctrination because of the controlled environment it uses, and more than Christian conversion because it does not rely solely on personal decisions and personal choices.

This is not to say that every person involved in the Unification Church is brain-washed. Some accept the theology because they agree with it. Nonetheless, the procedure is used in conjunction with the teaching to reinforce it and bring about one's accepting it.

De-programming, on the other hand, is merely the above procedure in reverse.[13] The method is the same with the exception of those abducted in some manner (their willingness develops in the controlled environment). The content used is totally different. Instead of hearing good things continually about Rev. Moon, for example, they now hear bad things continually. As one de-programmer expressed it, "It's fighting fire with fire."

One word of distinction should be noted here. De-programming is not Christian conversion. In the former the old pattern or program is broken, creating a religious vacuum in that life which is not filled. Thus a few of those de-programmed have returned to the former religious movement. The Bible describes this procedure and its problem in Matthew 12:43-45

> Now when the unclean spirit goes out of a man, it passes through waterless places, seeking rest, and does not find

it. Then it says, I will return to my house from which I came; and when it comes, it finds it unoccupied, swept, and put in order. Then it goes, and takes along with it seven other spirits more wicked than itself, and they go in and live there; and the last state of that man becomes worse than the first.

The latter, Christianity, differs in that the Holy Spirit comes into that person's being and begins the process of recreation. This happens when that person accepts Jesus as Lord and Savior.

Certainly Rev. Moon has founded a vibrant religious movement. One might describe it as an army of young people doing his bidding and spreading his message. The history of the Unification Church as well as that of Rev. Moon is marked with controversy, and further investigation is still needed in some areas. But, in the midst of that history, a strange theology was formulated around which the Unification Church was built. It is that theology which we need to examine next, for it provides the basis for all their practices. Throughout this section, glimpses of this theology have been revealed in the various experiences, encounters and problems. Once you note the theology, then some of the aspects of this history will take on even more significance. Then also you will know what it is they are trying to get you to believe and become involved in.

2
Moon's Theology Discerned

"But we believe in God and we love Jesus." How frequently I have met followers of Rev. Moon who have made just that statement. In fact, their conversations were punctuated with similar biblical phrases.

Perhaps you have never spoken to a member of the Unification Church. But if you have, did you happen to notice how "Christian" their statements appeared to be? Maybe you have attended one of Rev. Moon's lectures or have received literature published by the Unification Church? Did you notice the abundance of biblical terms and phrases used, such as born again, salvation, sin, only one God, one Christ, one Bible, Satan is the ruler of this world, and the day of the Second Coming of Christ?

In the midst of all this "Christian" terminology, many have become confused and some even fooled as to exactly what Rev. Moon and the Unification Church believe and teach. There is a reason for this confusion. It stems from the fact that they use biblical phrases and words; but it lies particularly in the way those who hear them attempt to interpret and understand those terms.

Let me illustrate this problem for you. One day while on my way to the New York Public Library, I noticed a small gathering of people. They were grouped around a young lady who, with the aid of a blackboard, was lecturing them on how science supported theology. She was a member of the Unification Church. I stood in the back of the group and listened for a while, occasionally observing the audience. Finally an elderly lady, who had been there longer than I, turned and said to me, "They sound Christian to me. After all, they do talk about God and Jesus, and seem to have a real zeal and love for the Lord." And with that she left, absolutely convinced that what that follower of Rev. Moon was saying was Christian.

There is a lesson to be learned from this episode. It has to do with the process she used to arrive at her conclusion. You see, she listened to the message and she heard familiar terms, Christian terms, but she made one great mistake. She interpreted those terms with her definition, thereby making what that young lady said Christian. She made no attempt to discern what that follower of Rev. Moon meant by those terms, and thus saw no difference. I'm sure if that member of the Unification Church had been pressed theologically, that woman would have seen a difference.

Lest we make the same error, let us begin by noting what a term or word is. In its basic form it is a linguistic symbol. The word God consists of three elements: G-o-d; the word Jesus, of five: J-e-s-u-s. What one means in using these words or linguistic symbols depends on the content one gives to them and/or the context in which one uses them. Therefore in order to know and understand what a person means when using a word, as in the case of this follower of Rev. Moon, we must understand what they mean by it first, and then compare that to what we mean by those terms. Only then can we discover whether they are really the same.

This language problem is precisely what the great Apostle Paul had in mind in 2 Corinthians 11:13-15, in which he vividly presents the fact that there are those who present "another Jesus," who represent "another gospel," and who impart "another spirit." For our purposes, we will only consider Paul's warning regarding "another Jesus." (The same could be demonstrated regarding "another spirit" and "another gospel.")

Virtually every religious movement in America today mentions Jesus Christ. In fact, He is an integral part of their theologies. They all use the same word Jesus, but do they all mean the same by it?

Consider some of these religious movements, noting carefully that each one presents Jesus, but with a different meaning. The Jesus of Christian Science is a divine ideal or principle, inherent within every man, and Jesus is its supreme manifestation; while the Jesus of the Jehovah's Witnesses is Michael the Archangel, prior to his divesting himself of his angelic nature and appearing in the world as a perfect man, as "a god." The Jesus of Mormonism is one god among many, while the Jesus of Spiritism is a pantheistic manifestation of Deity. The Jesus of Bahai is one of nine human messengers, while the Jesus of Meher Baba is one of many personifications or incarnations of God. The Jesus of Hinduism is one of many great teachers or gurus, an Avantaric form of Deity, while the Jesus of Christianity is the unique incarnation of God, "God manifested in the flesh." Each of the above religions use the same word Jesus. They all speak and teach about Jesus. Yet every one of them presented a different doctrine as to who He is. They all use the same word and they all mean something completely different by it.

Therefore it is absolutely imperative that we understand what people mean when using theological words. Dr. Young Oon Kim, professor of systematic theology and world religions at Unification Theological Seminary, makes this very point in the beginning of her book *Unification Theology & Christian Thought.* She says that in order to understand or even attempt to understand theology, one must first begin by understanding what is meant by the word "God." [1] In fact all Unification literature regarding theology begins with the attempt to understand God through the creation, and then continues to build its theology on that doctrine.[2] The importance of starting with an understanding of the word God is best stated by Dr. Emil Brunner, whom Dr. Kim quotes and is in agreement with on this point. "Indeed if one rightly understands that which the Bible means by the Creator, he has rightly understood the whole Bible. Everything else is involved in this one word."[3] But, just as there are many concepts of Jesus, as noted above, so also there are many diverse concepts concerning God. Thus it is imperative to understand what Rev. Moon means by the word God. After all, it is the initial difference between a right and a wrong understanding of theology. When he speaks of God, who or what is his God? Likewise, when he uses the name of Jesus, who is his Jesus?

In order to discover this and to know and understand his theology (that which is presented in *Divine Principle* and taught by the Unification Church), we must take care to interpret his words and phrases in his theological context, using only the content which he gives to them. This is not the easiest task because his theology is eclectic in nature, and occasionally contains his own unique terminology which one must understand in order to perceive his theology.

The following is Rev. Moon's basic theology in simplified fashion. It is not meant to be comprehensive or overly detailed, but merely a broad general outline constructed from the various writings of the Unification Church according to selected categories. To help understand clearly what he is saying, and at the same time to distinguish it from what he is not saying, his theology has been placed in contradistinction to the theology of the Bible. (Since Rev. Moon seems to indicate, at least publicly, that his theology is a continuation of biblical theology, we will continue to examine this "relationship" all the way through this book, using the historic orthodox position of Christianity as the basis.)

I. Who or What is God?

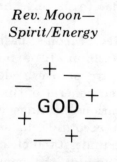

Rev. Moon—
Spirit/Energy

Christianity—
Spirit

GOD

FATHER HOLY SPIRIT

SON

Ultimately God is an invisible essence manifesting dual qualities —spirit and energy from which all existence generates.[4] Thus, with regard to the creation, God is set forth as "perpetual, self-generating energy."[5] As Dr. Kim states, "The energy, the force behind all matter, is God's external form...."[6] God also manifests dual polarity through paired relationships, such as male and female, positive and negative[7]—similar in

"God is Spirit" (John 4:24). He is personal, infinite, eternal and complete in himself. God is One, yet eternally exists as three persons: Father, Son and Holy Spirit (not dual polarity such as male-female, etc.); one unity (Tri-unity) in which love, fellowship, communication and interpersonal relationships exist always.

essence to the yin (male) and yang (female) principles of Taoist philosophy.[8]

Yet in this manifestation, God is also set forth as a personal God,[9] having consciousness, intelligence, love and purpose.[10]

II. How Did the World Come Into Existence?

Rev. Moon— Projected Out of God	*Christianity— Created Out of Nothing*

Creation, including the world, is the outward form of the invisible essence called

God created the world out of nothing. The creation is not God nor His outward form.

God.[11] The whole creation "is his body or outward form." [12] Thus God's creation activity is the emanation or projection, both physically and spiritually, of His essence. "God projected His heart and energy to form particles ... particles ... to form atoms ... atoms to form molecules, molecules to form minerals...." [13]

As Dr. Kim states: "He makes His presence k n o w n in the totality of c r e a tion which serves as His body, exemplifying His sovereignty and providing the outer form of His being." [14]

Note: Rev. Moon's theology is *Monistic*. It sets forth the explanation and existence of everything ultimately in one essence or substance which is God.

It is separate and distinct from His being. It did not emanate nor project from His essence (Gen. 1, 2; Ps. 33:6; Rom. 4:17; Heb. 11:3; etc.).

The creation declares the handiwork of God (Ps. 19:1) and one should realize from observing the creation that a personal God made it (Rom. 1:20), not that it is God or an extension of His being.

Note: Christian theology is *Theistic*. It sets forth the existence of a personal creator God as distinct in essence from the creation He made.

III. How Did Man Come Into Existence?

| *Rev. Moon—* | *Christianity—* |
| *Projection of God* | *Created by God* |

God projected from himself spirit beings in a sub-level existence, "a realm inhabited by spirits which have not yet grown to even the form level." [15] A spirit becomes a form spirit when it is born into a body in this world where it can develop a personality.[16] Each person has a spirit man and a physical man.[17]

Initially two of these, Adam and Eve, began in the garden

Men and women are created in the image of God, but not as a part of God. Man is the creature; God, the Creator. This distinction is never blurred in the Bible. God, being external to creation and distinct from it, took the dust of the ground, breathed into it giving it life, and man was created (Gen. 2:7). Together with Eve, whom God fashioned from a part of man, Adam was

of Eden.[18] They, like men and women after them, are the "external and objective manifestations of the polarity of God," [19] an extension of God out in the physical world.[20] Each person is "one unique part of God's Infinite Nature." [21]

placed in the garden of Eden. It was there that God met with them and their fellowship was personal (Gen. 1-3).

IV. How Did Man Break His Relationship With God?

Rev. Moon— Fornication with Lucifer

Christianity— Disobedience to God's Commands

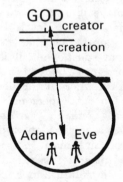

Adam and Eve were placed in the garden of

Adam and Eve were placed in the garden of

Eden to develop themselves through the stages of "formation," "growth" and "perfection." [22] The ideal goal was marriage once maturity (i.e. perfection) was attained.[23] It was at this point that "Adam and Eve would have formed a trinity with God" [24] and would have been able to "produce children free of inherited sin." [25] However, before they could attain perfection, Eve committed fornication with Lucifer. Lucifer and Eve became one in sexual union, causing the spiritual fall of mankind.[26] Eve, hoping to undo her action, persuaded Adam to to live with her as husband, even though he had not attained perfection either. This caused the physical fall of mankind.[27]

Through sexual union, Eve took on the Eden to care for it and to live there in perfect fellowship with God. They were told to be fruitful, multiply and fill up the earth (Gen. 1:28ff.). They were also told not to eat of one tree in the garden. However, Adam and Eve chose to disobey God. Their sin, according to God, was: "Have you eaten of the tree of which I commanded you not to eat of?" (not "Did you commit fornication with Lucifer?" See Genesis 3:11). Eve responded by saying, "The serpent deceived me and I ate" (not "The serpent deceived me and I committed fornication." See Genesis 3:14). This initial act of disobedience in eating of that which God had forbidden has affected the entire course of human history (Gen. 3:14-19; Rom. 5:15, 17; etc.). Man's basic problem

sinful characteristics of Lucifer, and Adam received these sinful characteristics through his sexual union with Eve.[28] Thus the entire course of human history deviated from the "divine principle" of maturing to perfection first, then marrying and producing perfect children.[29]

is that he has sinned before a holy and righteous God, thus alienating himself from his Creator in his heart and mind. Even today man continues to rebel against God and disobey Him as did his original parents, Adam and Eve.

V. How Can Man Become Right With God?

Rev. Moon—Jesus Failed in His Mission

Christianity—Jesus Triumphed in His Mission

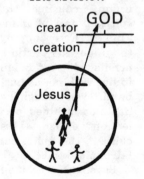

Salvation is basically the undoing of the results of the Fall. The individual has to be restored and perfected, and then enter into a marriage relationship and produce perfect children.[30] To accomplish this, a Messiah or a Christ is needed.[31]

Historically, Jesus the Messiah came in Adam's place to restore mankind. He was not Deity; " . . . it is a great error to think Jesus was God Himself." [32] Jesus on earth "was a man no different from us except for the fact that He was without original sin." [33]

Jesus' purpose in coming was to take a bride in Eve's place, marry and produce p e r f e c t children.[34] By the example and power of his family, other perfect families would be formed until

Salvation is exclusively God's provision for our sins through the death of His Son on Calvary's cross. Man cannot attain it, work for it or buy it. It is a free gift. One must recognize his condition before God as a sinner, confess his sins to God, believe that Jesus died in his place on the cross as payment for his sins (Jesus himself being without sin), and trust in Jesus Christ alone for a right relationship with God (Gal. 2:16; Eph. 2:8-9).

Historically, God took the initiative in the incarnation or Christ's first coming to redeem mankind. Jesus was fully God and fully man (Isa. 7:14; 9:6; John 1:1; 5:18; 10:30; etc.). Jesus' death was to pay the price for our sins. The Old Testament sacrificial system, along

the whole of society was restored and in line with God's purpose.[35]

Jesus *failed* in His mission. He was crucified before He could marry.[36] It was never God's predetermined purpose that He die.[37] It was the failure of John the Baptist that was "the major cause of the crucifixion of Jesus."[38] Because of this, God allowed Jesus to die. "Satan invaded the physical body of Jesus and crucified him."[39]

Jesus was resurrected from the dead as a spirit man, thus redeeming man spiritually.[40] At this point God could claim the souls of men, but could not give redemption to the body.[41] Jesus failed to redeem man physically.[42] Therefore physical restoration is still to be ac-

with numerous passages in both the Old and New Testaments, states that the Messiah had to die (Isa. 53; Ps. 27:13-18; Heb. 9:1ff.; 10:1ff.; etc.). Marriage was not the goal and His death was not a mistake (Acts 2:23). It was predetermined that God would provide salvation in this way and offer it as a free gift to all who would accept His Son Jesus as Lord and Savior (Rom. 5:8-11; Gal. 1:14).

His bodily resurrection from the dead guarantees that He has redeemed man totally (physically and spiritually), and His return to this earth one day will bring about this completion in the lives of His children (Rom. 8:23-4; 1 John 3:2-3; 1 Cor. 15:1ff.; etc.).

complished by another Messiah at the Second Advent.[43]

Rev. Moon—	*Christianity—*
Another Messiah	*Jesus Returns*

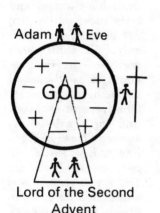

Lord of the Second Advent

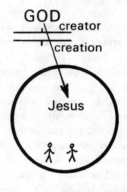

"The Lord of the Second Advent is to be born on the earth as the King of Kings."[44] We are not to expect the return of Jesus himself,[45] but another Messiah—a man who will be born in Korea.[46] (Rev. Moon

Because Jesus rose bodily from the dead, He lives today and is returning to this earth one day from heaven (not born as a man) to consummate His plan for the ages (Acts 1:11; 1 Thess. 4:13-17; Rev. 20:1ff.). Redemption, both spiritu-

was born in Korea.) He will be confirmed as the Messiah through the spirit world.[47] (Rev. Moon was confirmed in this manner.)

Though one may have his spirit man perfected by believing in Jesus, it will not help his physical man. Thus the Lord of the Second Advent will provide additional revelation[48] (Rev. Moon has a new revelation) which will enable the physical man to be perfected, thus completing the work of salvation.

A new age dawned in 1960: "At that time, the marriage of the lamb prophesied in the 19th chapter of Revelation took place. Thus, the Lord of the Second Advent and His Bride became the True Parents of mankind. ..."[49] (1960 happens to be the year in which Rev. Moon mar-

al and physical, is complete in Him. We receive this completion at the resurrection when Jesus returns (1 Cor. 15:20ff.), when we shall be like Him in the sense that we shall have a soul and body incapable of sin: not earthly, but heavenly. We shall reign with Jesus in His kingdom for a thousand years here on earth. The present heavens and earth will be destroyed. New heavens and a new earth will be created, where those who love Jesus shall live forever in His presence and fellowship.

ried his present wife Hak-Ja Han.) This Messiah will establish the perfect family, the task that Jesus never fulfilled.[50] Other perfect families will be formed, which will produce a perfect society that will spread to the entire world.[51]

In the 1980s the new Messiah will be revealed to the world (it appears that Rev. Moon is that person). When he declares the Kingdom, the life spirits of those who have lived before will join the followers of Rev. Moon so that they can develop into divine spirits.[52] Evil people will go through a similar reincarnation procedure.[53] The law of Karma is operative in this procedure, for "if any arrive in the spirit world with unpaid debts, they will have to work to assist perhaps the very ones they hurt in order to

There is no "Third Adam" or "New Messiah" needed, for what was effected by the disobedience of the first Adam in the garden of Eden was remedied by the Second Adam, Jesus Christ. Everyone who accepts Jesus as his personal Savior and Lord has right standing before God, and is assured of an eternal relationship with Him. Those who reject Him, at death are placed into Hades. At the second resurrection these will be cast into the Lake of Fire. At death this means eternal separation from God in a

pay what they owe." [54]

All the religions of the world will be unified,[55] which will bring about unification among all peoples.[56] Everyone will eventually be saved and perfected. The earth will be restored through the efforts of science.[57]

place of conscious torment (Rev. 20:13ff.; Matt. 8:11-12; 13:42-50; Luke 16:19-31; 2 Pet. 2:17; Jude 13; etc.).

"But as many as received him [Jesus Christ], to them gave he the right to become the children of God" (John 1:12).

It is obvious from the above that Rev. Moon's theology and that of the Unification Church has a unique definitive content all its own, and that it is quite different from biblical theology. From the initial differences of the Creator and the creation right down to the end-time product, they are two separate and distinct theologies.

Interestingly, though, members of the Unification Church generally attempt to stay away from these differences, at least initially in their contacts with outsiders. While speaking one night in a church in New Hampshire, a pioneer of the Unification Church was in the audience. After the meeting was over, he told me who he was and informed me that he had come into that town to develop a Unification center.

After some general conversation, I began to probe some theological areas. I asked him why he had accepted Rev. Moon's theology as true. He told me, "Because it clarifies everything in the *Bible*; it's the fulfillment of what the *Bible* teaches."

I asked him to consider a few areas of theology, comparing what the *Bible* stated and what the *Divine Principle* stated, and then to tell me honestly how the *Divine Principle* clarified or fulfilled the teachings of the *Bible*. The *Bible* states: "For in him [Jesus] all the fulness of Deity dwells in bodily form," [58] while the *Divine Principle* states that Jesus "can by no means be God Himself." [59] The *Bible* states that Jesus was "delivered up by the predetermined plan and foreknowledge of God," [60] while the *Divine Principle* states that it was not God's plan for Jesus to die.[61] The *Bible* states that Jesus rose bodily from the dead: Jesus said, "A spirit does not have flesh and bones as you see that I have," [62] while the *Divine Principle* states that Jesus did not rise bodily from the dead, but as a spirit man.[63] The *Bible* states that "this Jesus, who has been taken up from you into heaven, will come in just the same way as you have watched him go into heaven," [64] while the *Divine*

Principle states that Jesus will not return physically to this earth to set up His kingdom.[65] "How would you explain these statements?" I asked him. His reply was, "I'm really sorry. I don't know very much about the Bible." (Sometimes this is just a polite way of saying, "I'm not really interested in what you're saying.") And still he believed that the *Divine Principle* was a clarification or fulfillment of the teachings of the Bible.

Upon what basis could such an understanding be held? Certainly anyone can see that the *Divine Principle* neither clarifies nor fulfills what the *Bible* teaches. *It denies what the Bible states.* In fact, the *Divine Principle* is a rejection of all previous theological systems and world religions.

On another occasion a member of the Unification Church considered the differences between the *Divine Principle* and the *Bible* and merely dismissed it by saying, "You're a Fundamentalist. You take the Bible too literally." (This answer has been ingrained in them from the *Divine Principle*, which states that Christians today "are captive to scriptural words... according to the limits of what the New Testament words literally state." [66]) I replied, "That's quite a charge; but is what you claim really so?" "When you read a piece of literature," I continued, "what procedure do you use to understand it?" After quite a long roundabout explanation (in which he never did give a final answer), I said to him, "Look at it this way. When any person writes something, he or she writes it with only one meaning in mind. True?" He thought for a moment and then said, "Yes." "Then the interpretation of any document or piece of literature, be it a fragment of some pre-Socratic philosopher or a page from some medieval mystic, has as its goal the recovery of the exact meaning of the author. Right?" He replied, "Right." "And in order to discover that meaning we must use proper literary, historical and grammatical principles." [67] He agreed.

I opened up my Bible and said, "Consider the Luke 24 passage, verse 39. First of all, Luke's purpose in writing is historical—a factual account of what occurred (Luke 1:1-4). He lived at that time, knew the people involved and had access to all of the facts and could check them out. He was a physician, and thus a man of learning. Secondly, the occasion of this verse is after the death of Jesus; the context, the fright of the disciples who, having seen Jesus, thought He was a spirit. Jesus' reply to that was that 'a spirit does not have flesh and bones as you see that I have.' In fact, as you read further on, He even ate broiled fish which substantiates what He said about His bodily resurrection. Thirdly, we also have other historical evidence which corroborates the factuality of Luke's account, the statement of Jesus, and the fact that He rose bodily from the dead."

At this point I asked him if he saw any evidence or anything that would provide a different interpretation. He said, "No." I asked him, "Is that what Luke had in mind when he wrote his gospel, that Jesus rose bodily from the dead?" Finally he admitted it was so, and then concluded with the statement, "But the Bible is wrong there." The final position we came to is that a proper interpretation of the *Bible* and the *Divine Principle* will only yield the conclusion that these are two separate and distinct theologies and that both cannot be right. The discussion now settled on which was true.

The response of the members of the Unification Church in the above encounters can easily be understood when one realizes that they have been taught those statements in their training and believe them because the Unification Church taught it. Rev. Moon himself instructs his church leaders: "Until our mission with the Christian church is over, we must quote the Bible and use it to explain the Divine Principle. After we receive the inheritance of the Christian church we will be free to teach without the Bible." [68] Though it may not be the nicest way to express it (I'm a fisherman at heart), it appears from the above that the Unification Church uses the Bible as bait to draw one into its Unification theology which is totally different from the Bible. (I just think of that big old trout looking at my bait, thinking he's going to get a fat juicy worm dinner. Hopefully he ends up with the hook, something totally different from what he expected.) Once the bait is uncovered, then you see the hook—a different theology all together.

On still other occasions, members of the Unification Church have used the theme of unification in their approach. "Wouldn't it be nice if we could all get together; if the world was one big happy family?" Of course this is purported to be the mission of the new Messiah, the Lord of the Second Advent.[69]

Is Rev. Moon's theology really that in which all of Christianity as well as all of the world's religions can find fulfillment? As you compared his theology with that of Christian theology earlier in this chapter, did you see any areas of agreement? Is there any theology which could provide a common basis for all religions?

Certainly it is true that religions have something in common, or else the generic term would not exist. However, the closer one approaches an unarguable common denominator, the closer one comes to pure formality. (Try this with the dog category and see if you can come up with one dog which would be expressive of all the others.) The only theology that could provide a broad enough basis to include all other religions and thus unify them would be a theology that said nothing. A theology which unites all of the religions of the world is simply nonexistent.

Furthermore, the theology of Rev. Moon and that of Christianity, when compared to each other, leaves us with two complete and diverse systems in and of themselves.

They cannot both be true. The logical impossibility of this rests upon the de facto character of these two theologies themselves. To illustrate: Jesus said, "I am the way, the truth and the life: no man comes to the Father, but by me." [70] Peter states of Jesus: "Neither is there salvation in any other: for there is no other name under heaven given among men, whereby we must be saved." [71] Since Christianity and the *Bible* teach that Jesus Christ is the sole source of human salvation, and Rev. Moon and the *Divine Principle* teach that a future Messiah is to be the sole source of salvation, they cannot both be true. One denies the other. That is why Rev. Moon and the Unification Church teach that Jesus failed in His mission.

Unification theology is not the unifier of all of the world's religions nor of Christianity. It is the rejection of all of them. It presents the option of choosing Rev. Moon and rejecting all others. In private meetings Rev. Moon has stated, "God is now throwing Christianity away and is establishing a new religion." [72] Many times Rev. Moon has told his listeners— Protestants, Roman Catholics and Jews— that "they will have to make a choice" between their original faiths and his church.[73] One of Rev. Moon's spokesmen, "God's Colonel" Bo Hi Pak, while lecturing to several thousand Bostonians at Hynes Auditorium in July of 1974, spoke out against Billy Graham ("He can't tell you how the Messiah is coming."), Christian churches ("They keep watching for big signals from the blue sky."), and others.[74] These were all presented as though they were foolish attempts, and then the theology of Rev. Moon was set forth as truth.

There's no getting around it. Rev. Moon's theology is separate and distinct from Christian theology—they are mutually exclusive. You are left with the ultimate decision. Jesus would have you choose Him and reject Rev. Moon. Rev. Moon would have you reject Christianity and accept him.

To determine which theology is worthy of our credence and allegiance requires serious attention to Pilate's question "What is truth?"[75] Which of these theologies is true? Which presents the true doctrine of God and of Jesus Christ? With this in mind, we need to examine the claims of Rev. Moon and his theology in the light of the evidence to see whether it is truth.

One day while visiting the Unification Theological Seminary in Barrytown, a young lady who had been a member of the church for about six years said to me, "We both love Jesus, and that's the important thing." I pointed out that the Jesus of the Unification Church whom she believed in was different from the Jesus of the Bible whom I believed in. The object of our faith, belief and devotion was different. Her look exhibited the common response, "Why all this semantical nonsense? What does it really matter?" She replied, "You're familiar with the Bible. Jesus said, 'By their fruits you shall know them.' " [76] And with that she told me how much good the Unification Church was doing, how they were (at that time) cleaning up the streets in Manhattan, and the like. I pointed out that she should read the next few verses of that passage in Matthew 7 to note the all important issue: "Not every one who says to me, Lord, Lord, will enter the kingdom of heaven. . . . Many will say to me in that day, 'Lord, Lord, Look at all the good works we did in your name [my paraphrase]." [77] "Notice Jesus' response," I said, "to these 'good people.' 'I never knew you. Depart from me, you who practice lawlessness.' " [78] "You see," I continued, "the most important issue is a correct understanding of Jesus Christ and a personal relationship with Him as your Lord and Savior. All of the fruits or good works mean nothing if you miss this point."

Moon's Claims Examined

"With the fulness of time, God has sent His messenger to resolve the fundamental questions of life and the universe. His name is Sun Myung Moon." [1]

These words from the *Divine Principle* express the great expectations of the Unification Church and the claims of its founder, Rev. Moon. But how do we know they are true? How do we know that Rev. Moon is not a man deluded by visions of power and grandeur, or a fraud living luxuriously off those foolish enough to follow him and support him, or one deceived by a very clever evil supernatural power—Satan himself? Surely these are viable alternatives. How do we know which of these is true?

Questions like these were asked of several members of the Unification Church. Once the initial reaction was overcome, the general responses were reiterations of Rev. Moon being a messenger of God. As one young lady stated it: "I *know* beyond a shadow of a doubt that Rev. Moon is God's messenger and that his revelations are true." This answer would be fine if the question was "Do you believe Rev. Moon is a messenger of God?" But it certainly does not answer *how* you know this is so. If you repeat the question or rephrase it, stressing *why* they had accepted his claims and theology as true, you will get the following responses: "He has confirmation from the spirit world," "Science proves that his theology is true," and "He has the true understanding of the Bible."

The importance of this approach is that if someone or some religious movement calls on us to give our total allegiance to them, then it should have the evidence to back up all claims made and demonstrate its truthfulness in an objective fashion. It should not have to rely on thought control or "indoctrination" as is implemented in the Unification centers. If it cannot demonstrate its truthfulness objectively, then it would be foolish to give our lives over to such a person or group. We would be following that which is false in a blind faith.

From the above responses, some claims regarding Rev. Moon and also some evidence for his theology has been gathered and categorized. These are the ones we want to examine in this section. Bear in mind that these are claims and evidence presented by the Unification Church. If Unification theology is supported by these, then it should be seriously considered and accepted as true. If it is not supported, then it should be rejected.

The place to begin is with the *Divine Principle*'s claim that Rev. Moon is a messenger of God. This is a claim he himself makes continually, and one which his followers also set forth. This can be tested as there are several criteria set forth which would determine whether or not one is a messenger of God. After all, if Rev. Moon is to be the fulfillment of the Judeo-Christian religion as it is claimed,[2] bringing us the "completed testament" regarding that which is presented in the Old and New Testament,[3] then he must meet the qualifications of such a messenger in that religion or historic faith of which he claims to be an extension. In the list of qualifications for the Lord of the Second Advent, the Unification Church itself states that this must be so. In the *Divine Principle Study Guide* the Lord of the Second Advent must come "on behalf of God," the center of which "has been placed in Judeo Christianity. Therefore the work of the Lord must be based on this [Judeo Christianity] . . . ." [4] The context is explicit. If anyone does not meet the requirements of this basis as set forth in the Bible (that is the basis of Judeo Christianity), then that person could not be the Lord of the Second Advent.[5] If this is true of the Lord of the Second Advent, then it must also be true of Rev. Moon. With this in mind, let us look at these requirements as set forth in the Judeo-Christian Scriptures, the Bible.

First of all, a messenger of God must be in agreement with the previous divine revelation (the Old and New Testament) regarding the God he presents. The Bible specifically warns us in Deuteronomy 13:1-5 to watch out for self-proclaimed messengers of God because there are those who would lead us to follow and worship other gods than the one true God of the Bible. It should never be assumed that such a person will necessarily tell you that this is what he intends, for an entirely different religion may be constructed around orthodox terminology. Unification theology does exactly this, as we have already seen.

Does Rev. Moon and the Unification Church believe in and teach about the same God as the One portrayed in Judeo Christianity as set forth in the Bible? As we have already seen in the previous section, the doctrine of God expounded by Rev. Moon is vastly different from that of biblical theology. The doctrine of creation accentuates the total differences, for in the Bible God brings the creation into existence out of nothing, while in Unification theology the creation flows or projects itself out of God's being or essence, so that it is part of God. Thus Rev. Moon's doctrine of God is totally incompatible with and different from that of the Bible.

The Unification Church might attempt to avoid this conclusion by claiming that the doctrines of God and creation presented in the previous section and used in this comparison are not those of the historic Christian Church. (The Unification Church does stress Christianity when speaking of this Judeo Christian basis.) They might also point to the diversity of Christendom through the ages with its interpretations and doctrines and claim that it would be impossible to come up with only one orthodox position.

It is true that Christianity has had its divisions along cultural lines and even over doctrinal points. No one would deny this. However, these divisions have never precluded the broad doctrinal agreement of what the late C. S. Lewis called *Mere Christianity*. Here we find tremendous historic agreement.

The Christian Church of all ages has set forth the same basic doctrines which include the doctrines of God and creation used in the previous section and in the above comparison. These very doctrines, held by all orthodox believers, are expressed in the ecumenical creeds throughout church history. As noted Church historian Philip Schaff writes: "Almost all the creeds of the first centuries, especially the Apostles' and the Nicene, begin with the confession of faith in God the Father Almighty, Maker of heaven and earth, of the visible and the invisible." [6] Of course one might ask, as does the Unification Church, what the historic definition of "Maker of heaven and earth" is and how the early church interpreted it and understood it. Schaff answers this in stating that "God made the world, including matter, not, of course out of any material, but out of nothing. . . ." [7]

The church fathers also bear witness to this through the centuries.[8] Their understanding is similar to that of Augustine who wrote: "For Thou didst create heaven and earth, not of Thyself, for then they would be equal to Thine only-begotten, and thereby even to Thee. . . . Therefore, out of nothing didst Thou create heaven and earth." [9] It is true that at least one church father, Origen, held a peculiar view of creation, maintaining that it was eternal,[10] and that a few of the church fathers expressed the doctrine of creation by using Platonic forms. But not one church father held to the doctrine that God created the world out of himself, as the Unification Church believes.

The historic Christian Church would unitedly voice its rejection of Rev. Moon as a messenger of God simply on the basis that the God he presents is not the God of the Bible as historically defined and understood. Therefore Rev. Moon could not be of that tradition.

Secondly, the prophecies of a messenger

of God must always come to pass and be true. This test is set forth in Deuteronomy 18:22 where God says "that which the prophet speaks in the name of the Lord and the word does not happen nor come about, that is the word which the Lord has not spoken." In Isaiah 44:24-28 we see why this test will work. God promises that He will make fools of false messengers, but that He will uphold the predictions of His true messengers. One false prediction will prove that the message is not from God.

Though prophecies and predictions have not specifically been one of Rev. Moon's methods of presentation, nonetheless some of his statements could be understood as such, especially since they are revelations from God. One classic example of this was his support of President Richard Nixon in the midst of the Watergate crisis. On November 10, 1973, Rev. Moon took two weeks off from his tour of America for prayer and meditation regarding this.[11] On November 30, 1973, his message based on his revelations was published in leading newspapers. It was titled "Answer to Watergate: Forgive, Love, Unite." [12] Part of its message was this: "At this time in history God has chosen Richard Nixon to be Presi-

dent of the United States of America. ...
If God decides to dismiss this choice of His,
let us have faith that He will speak." [13]

From this message and its timing in the
midst of the Watergate investigation, one
would draw the conclusion that on the basis
of his revelations, Rev. Moon believed and
proclaimed Nixon's innocence. If you asked
his followers back then how they understood
this or were taught regarding this message,
they would tell you Nixon was innocent.
Shortly after all of this, Nixon resigned and
the entire subject was dropped and for-
gotten in the Unification Church.

Certainly the Unification Church could
work around this conclusion by interpreting
it differently. Hindsight always seems better than foresight. They simply point out
that the impeachment proceedings was no
solution to "Watergate morality," and that
good Americans should support their president and respect that office. It is true that
these points were included in Rev. Moon's
message.

John Lofland, in his book *Doomsday
Cult,* sets forth the claim of Rev. Moon that
the Lord of the Second Advent would be
revealed in 1967. This was not fulfilled and
now the date is 1980-81. But again the Uni-

fication Church can work around this since the book was withdrawn from publication shortly after its release.

Many believe that the great "prophetic test" for Rev. Moon will come in 1980-81 (1960 plus 21 years for Jacob's age) at which time he has prophesied that the Lord of the Second Advent will be revealed and the kingdom of heaven will be inaugerated.

As far as we are concerned in our context of examination, this prophecy is already in trouble (actually falsified) when examined in the light of historic Christianity. In order to make that prediction, Rev. Moon has to reject other statements and teaching in the Bible—doctrines given by God. Obviously to have another Messiah necessitates the failure of the first Messiah, Jesus. Likewise it is the rejection of the return of Jesus. There are many other doctrines which could be brought in here to illustrate the point that Rev. Moon's prophecy is contrary to the Bible and thus could not follow from that historic basis. Any messenger of God prophesying such a contradiction would automatically have been rejected.

Thirdly, a messenger of the true God must be in agreement with the previous divine revelation (the Old and New Testament) regarding the person and work of Jesus Christ. This test is clearly set forth in 1 John 4:2-3. Though the context is dealing with the Gnostic rejection of Jesus' coming in the flesh, the test is doctrinal in nature and centers around Jesus Christ. A wrong doctrine of Jesus, according to John, means a false messenger—one who is not of God. The New Testament stresses the fact that a true messenger of God will glorify Jesus as Deity, Redeemer and Coming King.

How does Rev. Moon view Jesus? Is it the same as that presented in the Bible? As we have seen in the previous section, Rev. Moon rejects the biblical teaching that Jesus is God, that He was victorious on Calvary's Cross in providing for our sins, that He rose bodily from the dead, and that He is coming again one day. There can be no doubt that Rev. Moon is in disagreement with the major doctrines regarding the person and work of Jesus Christ.

The Unification Church might object to this conclusion by again stating that the doctrines presented and used in the comparison are not the doctrines of historic Christianity. Let's consider the crucial question of Jesus' deity. All the church fathers believed this doctrine[14] and its truth is expressed in the various ecumenical creeds.[15] As Philip Schaff notes: "This doctrine [Jesus as the God-man and Redeemer of the world] was the kernel of all baptismal creeds, and was stamped upon the life, constitution and worship of the early church." [16] Henry Parry Liddon says, "If there be one doctrine of our faith which the martyrs especially confessed at death, it is the doctrine of our Lord's Deity." [17] In like manner the victory of Jesus on the Cross, His bodily resurrection from the dead, and His coming again to judge the living and the dead are essential to the life and teachings of the early church. They are taught by the church fathers, expressed in the creeds, and have been central to the doctrinal beliefs of Christianity through the ages.

The historic Christian Church would unitedly voice its rejection of Rev. Moon as a messenger of God on the basis of his rejection of the person and work of Jesus Christ as set forth in the Bible.

So far we have examined only one of Rev. Moon's claims—that he is a messenger of God. The criteria used to evaluate

this claim were three major areas presented in the Bible for such a test. There
are other areas such as his teaching of
"heavenly deception," which breaks the
ninth commandment: "Thou shalt not
bear false witness." A true messenger of
God would teach the Ten Commandments,
not break them and teach others to do likewise. Since Rev. Moon failed in all three
areas when tested, his claim to be a messenger of God in the historic tradition of
Judeo-Christianity cannot be substantiated.
The evidence does not validate his claim;
rather, it declares it to be false.

Another claim of Rev. Moon and the
Unification Church to consider is his confirmation from the spirit world. Rev. Moon
himself claims to have constant contact
with spirits and even claims to be an
"expert" on the spirit world. In fact,
through spiritism a person will know if he
is to be the Lord of the Second Advent.[18]
According to the Unification Church,
spiritism is also the way any person can
know that Rev. Moon is true. They claim
the spirits will document their leader.
"Those people who have sufficient communication with the spiritual world can receive direct confirmation concerning him.

Such a person is Arthur Ford, a well-known Philadelphia sensitive." [19] What they are saying is that if you visit your friendly spiritist, he will bear witness to Rev. Moon. Interestingly, several spiritists have already rejected Moon.

This spiritism may sound very good initially, but there are several problems which need to be considered. First of all, the Bible expressly forbids indulging in such spiritistic practices (see Lev. 19:31; 20:6-7; Deut. 18:11 and Isa. 8:19-20). Certainly no man of God would involve himself in these practices.

Secondly, the Bible presents an alternative understanding of spiritism. It is not the surviving personalities of dead people which are contacted in séances, but demons (created spirit beings which do evil and follow Satan) which impersonate the dead. If Satan can transform himself into an angel of light, he can certainly disguise himself as a dead saint (see 2 Cor. 11:14). Spiritism would also explain Rev. Moon's rejection of biblical theology.

Several years ago a noted authority of the cults, Rev. Walter R. Martin, wrote the following critique of spiritism:

Spiritism as a cult has been from its beginning in opposition to the Judaeo-Christian religions. In order for one to embrace its teachings, every major doctrine of the Christian faith must be rejected, including the inspiration and final authority of the Bible, the doctrines of the Trinity, the Deity of Christ, the Virgin Birth, Vicarious Atonement, and Bodily Resurrection of our Lord from the grave. The Biblical doctrine of salvation by grace alone, apart from the works of the Law, is anathema to spiritist theology which relies on progressive evolution or growth in the "spirit world," to attain final perfection.[20]

As you read the above synopsis of spiritism, did you see any similarities between Spiritistic Theology and that of Rev. Moon?

Thirdly, as William Peterson has observed, "Despite the fact that Moon claims to have talked with 'all the leaders in the Bible,' he still has a habit of contradicting them over and over again." [21] Of course the biblical interpretation of spiritism would explain why this is so. It was not the biblical leaders that he communicated with.

Fourthly, some of Rev. Moon's revelations contradict historical facts. For example, from the spirit world Rev. Moon concludes that Jesus did not rise bodily from the dead, but rather as a spirit man. Yet historic documents of that time period (the Gospels) and eyewitness accounts of people who lived then and saw Jesus in His resurrection body, record and report the fact that Jesus rose bodily from the dead.[22] To deny this is to deny history itself, and yet this is exactly what Rev. Moon is asking us to do on the basis of his subjective spiritistic revelation. Philip Schaff states the problem this way: "Before one can reason the [bodily] resurrection of Christ [Jesus] out of history, we must reason the apostles and Christianity itself out of history." [23]

Though people today may become caught up in movements that stress subjective experiences and revelations and thus be interested in what Rev. Moon says because of his revelations from the spirits, there are certain objective facts which should be considered from the above four points. The fact that history declares some of the information Rev. Moon has received from his revelations as false should tell us that his revelations are not trustworthy.

That these revelations contradict previous statements made by the same persons reinforces its untrustworthiness and make us wonder who or what it is he is contacting. The biblical interpretation of spiritism as demonism and not surviving personalities clearly expresses what Rev. Moon is involved in, explaining such elements as his non-biblical theology, deception and others. Finally, this is all condemned in the Bible which tells us that such spiritist involvement is totally untrustworthy.

The last claim we need to consider is that of science. That science supports their beliefs is basic to their approaches to theology as set forth in their literature and lectures. Even out on the street corners when you hear a member giving a short lecture, the starting point is usually the same—scientific methodology. This procedure is clearly set forth in the *Divine Principle Study Guide*: "Scientists first advance a hypothesis, and then they develop theories to explain the phenomena which they are studying. When they find that these theories explain the phenomena accurately, their hypothesis is defined as a theorum. We will apply the same method to prove the existence of God." [24]

In actuality though, the Unification Church goes far beyond even modern physics in its explanation of the creation. Whereas science today would express what is here in terms of energy and matter, Rev. Moon teaches that matter is varying forms of energy (as modern physics states) which is one of the forms of God (here physics departs)—i.e., in God's essence this energy exists, and matter is varying forms of that energy. Biblical theology would differ with Rev. Moon in that it teaches that God made the creation (energy and matter) out of nothing and not out of himself.

The Unification Church has attempted to demonstrate its "scientificness" in several other ways, the most notable being the International Conference of the Unity of the Sciences which it sponsors. Recently the fourth one was held at the Waldorf Astoria in New York City. Some 300 scientists and engineers, including 17 Nobel Prize winners, were invited. The stated purpose of the conference was to make some headway "towards the unification of science and religion." Others say it was a publicity move to gain worldwide attention and to give the appearance of scientific interests and teachings. Still others claim that Rev.

Moon just wanted the prestige of "rubbing shoulders" with all of these important people.

While at the Unification Theological Seminary one of the librarians remarked about the proceedings of this conference, indicating its importance. Perhaps it contains the Unification Church's view of the conference. To balance this it should be noted that two of the five co-chairmen, sociologist Amitai Etzioni and economist Kenneth Boulding, resigned prior to the conference.[25] One of those who did attend the conference wrote a report of that conference which is published in the *New Engineer*. He states that "most of the conferees remained distant from Moon's disciples and maintained no connection with his philosophy." [26]

Science is important to Rev. Moon because one of the preparations for the coming of the Lord of the Second Advent is that science must be at the highest level and harmonized with religion. While science is at its highest level, science has not harmonized itself with Rev. Moon's theology, nor does it verify his teachings.

To summarize, then, this section on the claims of Rev. Moon and the Unification

Church, we have examined three areas: Christianity, spiritism and science. Not one claim has been substantiated by the evidence, and beyond this there is evidence which contradicts the claims and theology of Rev. Moon. To test it further in other areas, especially in the realm of history (checking Rev. Moon's theological statements with that of biblical history), would only bring forth more evidence to the contrary. Thus the claims fail in their bid for credibility, leaving any seeker desperate for meaning and truth with no real basis for why one should give his life to Rev. Moon and the Unification Church. It also leaves us the alternative explanations presented initially. Perhaps Moon is deluded, or a fraud or demonically deceived. Whichever the case, he is not a messenger of God.

Because it has rejected the finished (completed) work of Jesus Christ and has replaced Him with the Lord of the Second Advent (another Messiah), the Unification Church bypasses offering Jesus Christ as a live option for your faith, your belief, your trust and your commitment. The Bible records the history of this One as the God-man who demonstrated His deity in His message, by His works and miracles and by His resurrection from the dead. He recognized the true condition of man as a "miserable sinner," estranged from God. This Jesus overcame the world, sin and death, thus concreting man's hope in eternal life—not through visions and spiritistic revelations, but by sacrificing His life on Calvary's cross for our sins and by rising bodily from the dead. One day He is coming to set up His kingdom. This very Jesus wants you to give your life to Him and let Him be your Lord and Savior—a faith determined on the combined basis of objective evidence and subjective commitment. Jesus Christ is man's only true faith and hope, and to reject Him as a result of someone's warping the content and message of the Bible is assuredly tragic blindness.

Conclusion

Throughout history, mankind has been introduced to religious movements and practices of all sorts. Certainly our generation is no exception. There has probably never been another period in the history of mankind in which so many of these have appeared at one time and with such diversity. The scene here in America has become a veritable clamor of religious confusion.

Somewhere along the line something has to be failing in order to produce so many religious offerings and such a massive interest in these. There is no doubt that our culture is at least partly to blame. Living in an age of rationalism in which everything can be reasoned out and explained has not provided the answers to man's problems. An age of scientific, medical and technolog-

ical profundity as we have today has not
solved man's problems nor alleviated his
fears. It hasn't told him who he is and the
purpose of life. War and violence continues,
while poverty and hunger increases. Families are crumpling. Human worth and dig-
nity appear to be at an all time low. The
future, if you listen to the prognostica-
tors (economic or whatever), looks bleak.
Is it any wonder today that so many people,
especially young people, are looking for so-
lutions anywhere they can find something?

But then too, since the quest today is
religious in nature, part of the failure must
include the churches. As Jan Karel Van
Baalen has pointed out in his book *The
Chaos of Cults:* "The cults are the unpaid
bills of the church." [1] Perhaps as a result of the acculturation of our age in which
churches have become rationalistic, cold
and logical, adopted materialistic values,
etc., many have turned from the church
because of its similarity in these areas to
the culture itself which they rejected.
Therefore they assumed that it did not have
the answers to their questions and problems. Surely this has happened in some
areas. Perhaps as a result of the de-
emphasis of the doctrinal aspects of Chris-

tianity along with its bearing on everyday life, many have been cut adrift from their nominal faith and discouraged by their previous shallow association with a pseudo-Christianity. These are the people who become prey for the cults in general, and in speaking to many members of the Unification Church, the reason so many have left churches to join with Rev. Moon.

Since it is people who are involved in the quest, we need to look at the individual person because he too is a part of this failure. The human nature of man is by its very constitution in a continuous state of rebellion against the authority of God and the truth of the gospel. Thus man by nature seeks anything else but the God of the Bible. It's unbelievable some of the things man would replace God with.

So into a world that has not solved man's problems, amidst churches which have been rejected by young people, to people who by nature are religious, some seeking the true God and others running from Him, comes Rev. Moon and his Unification Church. They have the proposed solution to everything. They want to restore the family unit as the basis of society. They are opposed to communism. Drugs, immorality and pornography are their enemies since these adversely affect both the individual and society. In a day of permissiveness, they offer structure complete with absolute authority. (Many young people today want to be told what to do.) They involve every person in the working of their program, and they promise to remake the world into a paradise and bring about perfection. They even offer a leader who is yet to be revealed—another Messiah who will accomplish all of this in a few years.

But, since the claims of Rev. Moon and the Unification Church cannot be substantiated and there is abundant evidence which contradicts what they say, the promise they offer will never become a reality. The foundation upon which the paradise was to be built is already false.

There is a lesson to be learned from this, for the Unification Church does offer some things which evidentally meet the needs of some of today's youth. Such areas as being a part of the community or group, every person working for the cause, active involvement, speaking out against evil and taking a stand on something, structure rather than an open situation, relating teachings so the average person can understand it, concern for the family unit, etc., the Christian Church would do well to consider in the light of the program they now offer to their youth as well as to those outside the church.

The Unification Church is part of a growing trend in America away from the established Christian Church and the historic teaching of the Bible. It is a challenge to Christianity to once again affirm the great principles and foundations of the Gospel of Jesus Christ, to communicate that gospel in language anyone can understand, to relate it to life itself so it is meaningful to every individual person in this generation, and to provide answers to the perplexing questions people are concerned with today. When the church fails to analyze itself in the midst of an ever increasing number of religious movements and practices, it misses the temper and mind of people. But more than that it loses its opportunity to deal with the needs of people at the very point when it might most readily have entered into them.

Rev. Moon and the Unification Church does not have the answer to man's dilemma. As Mr. Suto pointed out in his lecture on the "Practical Aspects of Training" at Barrytown:

In the Unification Church, many have joined and many have left, and few remain. We have lost many, many brothers and sisters. They believed Father was the Messiah; they received the *Divine Principle*. They made deep determination to sacrifice their entire lives, yet many left because we couldn't raise these members enough.[2]

Christianity does have the answer in Jesus Christ. As Jesus said in John 3:16, "God so *loved* the world that he *gave* his only begotten Son; that whosoever *believes* in him shall never perish, but *have* eternal life." Jesus Christ alone is "the way, the truth, and the life," and no one can come to God unless they come through Him (John 14:6).

Why I Left the Unification Church

by Michael Scott

"You will become completely claimed by Satan!" Feeling these words sink deeply into my heart, I said good-bye to the Unification Church forever. I had been saved as a child at the age of seven and had been baptized into a small Spirit-filled Baptist church. Throughout the following years, I had been an average church-going Christian. But during my latter high school days, I became more and more disillusioned because of the discrepancies I saw in the lives of professing Christians and soon stopped attending altogether. In my life, I lost all thought of Jesus and His church, even of God himself. My life took turns for the worse without God, including a drug-filled year at college and a short stint in the army.

After the army and a deep venture into the world of the occult, I came to New York City, carrying only a one-way ticket, luggage, and

$100—knowing no one. I worked at temporary jobs for two weeks, unable to find anything permanent. One Monday afternoon, as I came out of the New York Public Library on 5th Avenue, a clean-cut Japanese youth, speaking broken English, approached me and invited me to attend a lecture on the "Divine Principle," a revelation supposedly from God to Rev. Sun Myung Moon. Having nothing particularly important to do, I agreed.

Things moved so quickly that before I realized it, I found myself at Tarrytown late Friday night. I, along with approximately 50 other prospective "spiritual children," was awed.

I was brought into a packed room, overflowing with Moon posters, buttons, and friendly, smiling young people from all over the world. I was then led into a lecture hall, where I heard a lecture on "God's Providence of the Restoration of Human History." It was quite logical to my human understanding, and finally after quite a bit of coaxing, I agreed to attend a three-day seminar at upstate Barrytown the coming Friday.

The pace of the seminar was hectic. We rose at 7 a.m. on Saturday, had morning exercises, breakfast, and then attended lectures until 2 p.m. After lunch and recreation, we listened to lectures until after midnight, pausing only briefly for dinner at 9 p.m. The same schedule was followed on Sunday. When the lectures ended on Monday at 6 p.m., we were greeted by our "spiritual parents," who had come to urge us to join the Unification Church.

My resistance had been worn very low by averaging less than five hours sleep nightly, many hours of lectures, the spiritual atmosphere of Barrytown, and the warm friendliness and sincerity of everyone. All these factors, plus the logic and clarity of the Divine Principle, had overwhelmed me, and I was hooked.

The basic tenets of the doctrine were that the fall of man was the result of an illicit and immoral relationship between Eve and the Archangel Lucifer, and then in turn between Eve and Adam; and that Jesus did not come to die on the Cross, but rather to set up a worldly kingdom of heaven on earth. Instead, He failed His earthly mission and through the crucifixion could only offer spiritual salvation; therefore, He must return again, born of woman, to complete it. I was taught that among the signs to look for were (1) that Korea was the fatherland of the new Messiah, supposedly the new Israel mentioned in Revelation; (2) that the Messiah must be born between 1917-1930, according to Moon's historical periods comparison chart; and (3) the Messiah must come bearing a clarifying new revelation. I saw that Rev. Moon, born in Korea in 1920, and presenting the Divine Principle, just happened to fulfill the requirements.

My conviction that Moon was this new Messiah was reinforced the first time that I heard him speak, three days after I joined the "family." As he walked into the room, everyone bowed his/her head as if to worship his presence. He was referred to as "Father." Also, he and his third wife were called the "True Father and

Mother," or "True Parents," being the embodiment of this Messiah and his perfect, sinless bride.

I stayed with the church for nearly a year. During this time, I was on a mobile selling (fund-raising) team, traveling from Colorado to Oregon; on a mobile witnessing team in Washington, D.C., area; in church centers in New Rochelle, White Plains and Manhattan; and in extended training in Barrytown. I was very active, living sacrificially and humbly, doing only what "Father" said. We worked hard from 6 a.m. to midnight, finally getting to sleep at around 2 a.m., in sleeping bags on the floor in assigned rooms, men and women separate.

Close contact between the sexes was discouraged. "Brothers" and "sisters" found to be developing a close relationship were judged and chastised, usually compelled to take one or more cold showers daily, usually three minutes long, as a condition of repentance.

Our respect and humble obedience went to the older members, who had been through so much "persecution," paying the "indemnity" for all us younger members to accept the "truth." The very highest respect went to the "blessed sisters." A blessed sister was one who had been "blessed" in marriage to a brother by Rev. Moon. To obtain this she had to have a deep level of spiritual growth and belief in Principle and to have been in the family for at least three years.

To obtain the Divine Principle, hypothetically, the Completed Testament, the highest degree of truth, Moon had supposedly gone through great spiritual struggles, fighting his way through the spirit world from the depths of hell and battling with Satan, to the highest reaches of heaven, where all the spirit world acknowledged that he was the "Lord of Creation," the Messiah! Thereupon, every spiritual creature, even God himself, had bowed down and worshipped him!

In October 1974, most of the members underwent a seven-day fast. We were told by Moon that this was a hidden requirement for core membership in the Unification Church. Drinking only water, we continued our normal activities. Moon then proclaimed that we had symbolically paid all the indemnity for mankind's sins throughout history. Now, under him, we could march forward into "New History."

Moon continued that we would have to do more fund-raising in the future to restore the economic situation of the world. In order to successfully do this, we would have to work harder, sell harder, also that we could buy and "claim from Satan" the Ford Motor Company, Pan American Airlines and the Empire State Building. We would then establish a university, rivaling the Ivy League schools in academic standards, and found a newspaper larger and more influential than the New York *Times*.

These words struck something deep inside me. I began to see Moon as a very shrewd, evil man, seeking personal power and prosperity at any cost. While we pursued our very sacrificial life-style, he was living in a plush mansion in Irvington, New York—a mansion few members had access to because we were unworthy to even unloose the latchet of his shoes. We were told he was living as he did because he had to develop relationships with Senators, Congressmen, and other dignitaries. How unfitting it would be for the Messiah to greet them in modest surroundings. This was cited as one of the reasons that Jesus' mission was a failure.

It was continually emphasized that Rev. Moon was the embodiment of the Christ spirit. The word "Christ" comes from the Greek *Christos,* meaning Messiah, or Anointed One. The point that the *person* of Jesus, the Christ, was the central figure of the New Testament, rather than just the Christ spirit, was evaded. Jesus said we were to believe on His *name,* not just His title. As I secretly studied the Scriptures, this became more and more evident to me.

In prayer, the general procedure was to pray in the names of "Our True Parents." This was altered only if nonmembers were present. Then we would pray in the name of "Christ, Our Lord." I began to find it impossible to pray in their names. I was under a great deal of stress.

How could these people call themselves Christians and yet *blaspheme* the precious name of Jesus Christ our Savior, God's *only* begotten Son? I couldn't! I wouldn't!

I became very negative and bitter. For several weeks I feigned illness so that I would not have to participate in their witnessing or fund-raising. This allowed me to study the Bible more. In my studies, I became even more confident that this was not God's hope for man, but rather, Satan's. Sensing my inner turmoil, they openly accused me of committing some great sin. Therefore, my illness was God's judgment.

"We cannot lounge when the world needs to be restored," I was told. "You must return to God's service or leave. You will be completely claimed by Satan." I was ostracized and criticized beyond endurance.

On April 11 of this year (1975), I became desperate, reaching the point where I could no longer stay with them. In the hope of friendship or some small bit of consolation or help, I called a crisis telephone number. In explaining my situation, I was referred to Calvary Baptist Church in New York City. Minutely hoping to receive some advice or help, I visited the church, only to find God's love and forgiveness and open arms!

Through God's grace and Calvary Baptist Church, I found love, help and a new start. But most important, reconciliation to God! That very evening I left the Unification Church forever, I was not "claimed by Satan" rather I was "reclaimed by God."

God really blessed me for returning to Him. Within two days I found a job and soon after an apartment.

I pray that through this personal testimony someone else will be led to the true God through Jesus Christ, our wonderful Lord and Savior. Please join me in prayer for the Unification

Church members and members of all cults around the world, that they may also find a new start in God's blessed love and be completely claimed by Him.

Excerpts from *Master Speaks*

The Claims of Rev. Moon

"By the fulfillment of my mission, I fulfill the mission of Jesus and Moses." (*Master Speaks,* March and April, 1965, MS-1, p. 8)

"I have inherited the mission and the work, and succeed Jesus in this work. I am fulfilling what Jesus left undone." (*Master Speaks,* March and April, 1965, MS-3, p. 14)

"I have talked with many, many Masters, including Jesus, on questions of life and the universe and creation and God's dispensation, and many other things. They have subjected themselves to me in terms of wisdom. After winning the victory, they surrendered." (*Master Speaks,* March and April, 1965, MS-3, p. 16)

"What will Jesus' position be after the restoration is accomplished? Jesus will be the first and eldest son, because he was the only one who came to this world as the Son of God. *Do you mean God's eldest son, or the Master's?* The

meaning is the same." (*Master Speaks,* March and April, 1965, MS-4, p. 9)

"Jesus was born of a father and a mother, just as anyone else is, but in his case the Spirit of God was working also." (*Master Speaks,* March and April, 1965, MS-7)

"When you read the Bible, it appears as if Jesus knew everything. But he didn't. He did not know how the fall of man took place as clearly as we do." (*Master Speaks,* March and April, 1965, MS-1, p. 2)

" . . . I had to pay indemnity for what had been lost by Jacob, Moses and Jesus." (*Master Speaks,* March and April, 1965, MS-2, p. 3)

"I have paid a great amount of indemnity, and because of this I have the right to forgive another's sin." (*Master Speaks,* March and April, 1965, MS-3, p. 16)

"You know, for thirty years our movement has been delayed by the initial rejection I received when I first declared this message. Koreans deserve hell, so that nation must suffer. Christians all over the world deserve to decline, because they did not accept me." (*Master Speaks,* December 25, 1974)

* * * * *

"From now on, the work of restoration will be speeded up because the True Parents are now on earth. God can now lead you through them." (*Master Speaks,* March and April, 1965, MS-3, p. 10)

"As Christians, we prayed in the name of the Father, the Son, and the Holy Ghost or Holy Spirit. Now we should pray in the name of the True Parents." (*Master Speaks,* March and April, 1965, MS-3, p. 2)

* * * * *

"We are tigers to shake the whole world. We are great personages to change the whole world. Our stage is the whole world. The leading nation of the whole world is America and we want to shake America first." (*Master Speaks,* November 10, 1974)

"After our victory, after our triumph in this nation, I must build an ideal city or state in this nation. Then people will visit that place in chartered planes from all over the world, and if I am not able to do that, I will be a failure." (*Master Speaks,* July 29, 1974)

"Without your knowing, I have been using my P.R. members to win the minds of the Senators and Congressmen, and get them assembled. I am going to talk before those Senators and Congressmen soon. For six months' time, I have planted them for this purpose." (*Master Speaks,* September 29, 1974)

"After sending out our missionaries to 120 nations, we can influence those nations, and by having the youth of those nations mobilize, we can form a new United Nations." (*Master Speaks,* October 28, 1974)

* * * * *

"The Divine Principle . . . is truth in its fullest meaning, but not the Bible word by word. The Divine Principle clearly shows how the Bible is symbolic and how it is parabolic . . . The Bible is based upon the truth. The Divine Principle gives the true meaning of the secret behind the verse." (*Master Speaks*, March and April, 1965, MS-7(2), p. 1)

"Until our mission with the Christian church is over, we must quote the Bible and use it to explain the Divine Principle. After we receive the inheritance of the Christian, we will be free to teach without the Bible." (*Master Speaks*, March and April, 1965, MS-7, p. 1)

* * * * *

"I am a thinker. I am your brain." (*Master Speaks*, May 17, 1973)

Notes

Notes to Introduction

1. *Eternity,* April, 1976, p. 28.
2. See his letter to *Christianity Today,* July 5, 1974, p. 24.
3. *New York Times,* Sunday, February 15, 1976, p. 14.

Notes to Chapter 1

1. *DPA,* p. vii.
2. *Sun Myung Moon,* p. 6; cf. *Master Speaks,* March and April, 1976, MS-3, pp. 4ff.
3. *DP,* p. 16.
4. *Time,* October 15, 1973, p. 129.
5. As quoted in William J. Peterson, *Those Curious New Cults,* New Canaan, Conn: Keats Publishing Co. 1976, p. 250; cf. *Time,* June 14, 1976, p. 150 and Arao Arai, *The Madness of Japan,* Tokyo: Seison, 1975.
6. *Christian Century,* June 25, 1975, p. 647.
7. *DP,* p. 16.
8. E.g., UTCT, p. 234. Dr. Kim does not seem

to find *many* parallels between the two Babylonian Captivities as the *Divine Principle* states.

9. *The Way of the World,* January 1975,
p. 2.

10. John Cotter, "How Moon Wins Hearts
and Minds," *New York Daily News,* Tuesday,
December 2, 1975, p. 38.

11. *Time,* August 16, 1976, pp. 31ff.

12. *Time,* June 14, 1976, p. 50.

13. See Ted Patrick, *Let My Children Go,*
New York: Dutton, 1976, for accounts of de-
programming and their explanations.

Notes to Chapter 2

1. *UTCT,* p. 2.

2. E.g., *DP, DPA, DPSG, PC.*

3. *UTCT,* p. 2.

4. *DPSG,* p. 14.

5. *DPA,* p. 5; cf *DPSG,* p. 8.

6. *UTCT,* p. 7.

7. E.g., *DPA,* pp. 3, 5; cf. *DPSG,* pp. 13ff.
and *DP,* p. 25.

8. *DPSG,* p. 16; cf *DP,* pp. 26-7. Note the
differences which are pointed out between Unification theology and Taoist philosophy. While
some elements, such as the Sung-Sang and Hy-
ung-Sang and that which is involved in the
process to produce "all the creation," are different, *the overall system and framework is
identical.* In both cases, everything projects out
from God, dualism forms the basis for all manifestations, and everything finds its explanation
and existence in God's essence.

9. E.g., *DPSG*, pp. 30ff.

10. *DPSG*, p. 8.

11. *PC*, p. 13; cf. *DPSG*, p. 16 and *DP*, p. 25.

12. *DPA*, p. 2; cf. *DPSG*, p. 15; *DP*, p. 40 and *UTCT*, p. 7.

13. *PC*, p. 22; cf. *DPSG*, p. 24.

14. *UTCT*, p. 7.

15. *DPA*, pp. 24-5.

16. *DPSG*, pp. 46ff.

17. *DP*, pp. 60ff.

18. *DPSG*, pp. 62ff.

19. *DPA*, pp. 3, 11; cf. *DPSG*, p. 64.

20. *DPSG*, p. 36.

21. *PC*, p. 52.

22. *DPSG*, p. 38; cf. *DP*, p. 53.

23. *DPA*, p. 41; cf. *DPSG*, p. 26 and *DP*, p. 57.

24. *DPA*, p. 77; cf. *DPSG*, p. 26.

25. *DPA*, p. 41.

26. *DPA*, p. 38; cf. *DPSG*, pp. 81-3 and *DP*, pp. 72-3.

27. *DPSG*, pp. 83-4; cf *DP*, p. 72-3.

28. *DPA*, pp. 64-5; cf. *DPSG*, p. 83.

29. *DPA*, p. 77.

30. *DPSG*, p. 129.

31. *DPSG*, p. 129; cf. *DP*, p. 139.

32. *DPA*, p. 75; cf. *DPSG*, p. 192 and *DP*, pp. 211ff.

33. *DP*, p. 212; cf. *DPSG*, pp. 129, 194.

34. *DPA*, pp. 64-5; cf. *DP*, pp. 140-1.

35. *DP*, pp. 209-13.

36. *DPA*, pp. 64-5.

37. *DP*, p. 143; cf. *DPSG*, p. 133.

38. Rev. Sun Myung Moon, *Christianity in Crisis;* cf. *DPSG*, pp. 149-54 and *DP*, pp. 157ff.

39. *DPSG*, p. 138.

40. *DP*, p. 212.

41. *DPSG*, pp. 139, 165; cf. *DP*, pp. 147ff.

42. *DPSG*, p. 197.

43. *DPA*, p. 71.

44. *DP*, p. 510.

45. *DP*, pp. 500, 510.

46. *DP*, p. 520.

47. *DP*, p. 177.

48. *DP*, p. 179; cf. *DPA*, pp. iv, vii.

49. *DPA*, p. 196.

50. *Ibid.*

51. *DP*, pp. 184ff.; cf *DPSG*, p. 172.

52. *DPSG*, pp. 169ff.; cf. *DPA*, pp. 24-5 and *DP*, pp. 182ff.

53. *DPSG*, pp. 174ff; cf. *DP*, pp. 157ff.

54. *DPA*, p. 50.

55. *DPSG*, pp. 179 ff.; cf. *DPA*, p. 194 and *DP*, pp. 188ff.

56. *DP*, p. 194.

57. *DP*, p. 452.

58. Colossians 2:9.

59. *DP*, pp. 210-1.

60. Acts 2:23.

61. *DP*, p. 143.

62. Luke 24:39.

63. *DP*, p. 212.

64. Acts 1:11.

65. *DP*, p. 513.

66. *DP*, p. 534.

67. Mortimer J. Adler, *How to Read a Book*, New York: Simon & Schuster, 1940, sets forth

some basic principles for use with any literature. For a comprehensive basis regarding the principles used in interpreting the Bible, see William C. Lincoln, *Personal Bible Study,* Minneapolis, Minnesota: Bethany Fellowship, Inc., 1975.

68. As quoted in *Eternity,* April 1976, p. 27.

69. *DPA,* p. 194.

70. John 14:6.

71. Acts 4:12.

72. As quoted in *Time,* September 30, 1974, p. 68.

73. *Newsweek,* October 15, 1973, p. 54.

74. *The Boston Phoenix,* July 23, 1974, p. 10.

75. John 18:38.

76. Matthew 7:20.

77. Matthew 7:21-2.

78. Matthew 7:23.

Notes to Chapter 3

1. *DP,* p. 16.

2. E.g., *DP,* pp. 232-8; cf. *DPA,* p. vii and *DPSG,* pp. 163-73.

3. E.g., *DP,* p. 137; cf. *DPSG,* pp. 5-6.

4. *DPSG,* p. 167.

5. *Ibid.*

6. Philip Schaff, *History of the Christian Church,* Vol. II, p. 536.

7. *Ibid.,* p. 540.

8. E.g., Tatian, *Address to the Greeks,* 5; Irenaeus, *Adversus Haereses,* 2.10; Clement of Alexandria, *Stromata,* 5:14; and John Scotus Erigena, *Of the Divineness of Nature,* 3.5, 14.

9. Augustine, *Confessions,* 13.7.

10. Origen, *De principiis,* 1.3.10.

11. *New York Times,* November 30, 1973, p. 16.

12. *Ibid.*

13. *Ibid.*

14. E.g., Ignatius, *Ephesus,* 7.2; 15:3; 18:2; *Romans,* 3.3; 6.3; Athenagorus, *Plea for the Christians,* 10; Tertullian, *Against Praxeas,* 2; and Origen, *Contra Celsus,* 1. VIII, 67.

15. E.g., the Nicaeno-Constantinopolitan Creeds and Athanasian Creed.

16. Schaff, *op. cit.,* p. 545.

17. Henry Parry Liddon, *The Divinity of our Lord and Saviour Jesus Christ.* p. 406.

18. *DP,* 529ff.

19. *Sun Myung Moon,* p. 6.

20. Walter R. Martin, *Kingdom of the Cults,* Minneapolis: Bethany Fellowship, Inc., 1969, p. 212.

21. William Peterson, *op. cit.,* p. 259.

22. For a study of the historical method applied to Christianity, see John Warwick Montgomery, *History and Christianity,* Downer's Grove, Ill.: Inter-Varsity Press, 1969. This is also published in his *Where Is History Going?,* Minneapolis: Bethany Fellowship, Inc., 1969, chapters 2 and 3.

23. Schaff, *op. cit.,* Vol. I, p. 183.

24. *DPSG,* p. 1.

25. *Christian Century,* September 24, 1975, p. 812.

26. Cy Adler, "A Moon Shines on Science," *New Engineer,* Vol. V, No. 3, March 1976, pp. 39-41.

Notes to Conclusion

1. Jan Karel Van Baalen, *The Chaos of Cults,* Grand Rapids: Wm. B. Eerdman's, 1962, p. 390.

2. Mr. Suto, "Practical Aspects of Training," *120 Day Training Program,* p. 362. Mr. Suto blames this failure on lack of leadership, and called upon the members to become better leaders so these departures will not happen. As many ex-members have stated, the problem is not leadership, but the false claims and message of this movement, and the deception.

Bibliography

Materials by the Unification Church

Books

Divine Principle. Washington, D.C.: Holy Spirit Association for the Unification of World Christianity, 1973.

The Divine Principle Study Guide. Belvedere Tarrytown, N.Y.: Holy Spirit Association for the Unification of World Christianity, May 1, 1973.

Jones, W. Farley (editor). *A Prophet Speaks Today: The Words of Sun Myung Moon*. New York, N.Y.: HSA-UWC Pub., 1975.

Kim, David S. C. (Compiler). *Day of Hope and Review: Part I, 1972-1974*. Belvedere Tarrytown, N.Y.: Holy Spirit Association for the Unification of World Christianity, May 1, 1974.

Kim, Young Oon. *The Divine Principle and Its Application*. Belvedere Tarrytown, N.Y.: Holy Spirit Association for the Unification of World Christianity, n.d.

Kim, Young, Oon. *Unification Theology & Christian Thought*. New York: Golden Gate Publishing Co., 1975.

Kim, Young Whi*. *The Principle of Creation.* Belvedere Tarrytown, N.Y.: Holy Spirit Association for the Unification of World Christianity, March 15, 1973.

120 Day Training Program. Barrytown, New York: Holy Spirit Association for the Unification of World Christianity, n.d.

Unification Thought. New York, N.Y.: Unification Thought Institute, 1973.

Unification Thought Study Guide. New York, N.Y.: Unification Thought Institute, January 30, 1974.

Booklets

Rev. Sun Myung Moon. *Christianity in Crisis,* 1974.

Rev. Sun Myung Moon. *God Bless America,* 1976.

Periodicals

Leader's Address.

The Master Speaks (transcribed messages of Rev. Moon).

The Rising Tide (newspaper).

The Way of the World (magazine).

Materials About the Unification Church
Books

Arai, Arao, *The Madness of Japan.* Tokyo: Seison, 1975.

Cohen, Daniel, *The New Believers,* New York: Ballantine Books, 1975.

Ellwood, Robert S. Jr. *Religious and Spiritual Groups in Modern America.* Englewood Cliffs, N.J.: Prentice-Hall, 1972.

Lofland, John. *Doomsday Cult.* Englewood Cliffs, N.J.: Prentice-Hall, 1966.

Patrick, Ted. *Let My Children Go.* New York: Dutton, 1976.

Peterson, William J. *Those Curious New Cults.* New Canaan, CT: Keats Publishing, Inc., 1975.

The Religious Re-awakening in America. Washington, D.C.: U.S. News & World Report, Inc., 1972.

Booklets

J. Isamu Yamamoto. *The Moon Doctrine.* Downers Grove, IL: Inter-Varsity Press, 1976.